PLATEOSAURUS
AND OTHER DESERT DINOSAURS

by **Dougal Dixon**

illustrated by
Steve Weston and James Field

PICTURE WINDOW BOOKS
Minneapolis, Minnesota

Picture Window Books
5115 Excelsior Boulevard
Suite 232
Minneapolis, MN 55416
877-845-8392
www.picturewindowbooks.com

Printed in the United States of America.

Library of Congress Cataloging-in-Publication Data
Dixon, Dougal.
Plateosaurus and other desert dinosaurs / written by
Dougal Dixon ; illustrations by James Field, Steve
Weston ; diagrams by Stefan Chabluk ; cover art by
Steve Weston.
p. cm. — (Dinosaur find)
Includes bibliographical references and index.
ISBN 1-4048-0667-9
1. Dinosaurs—Juvenile literature. 2. Desert animals—
Juvenile literature. I. Field, James, 1959- ill. II. Weston,
Steve, ill. III. Chabluk, Stefan, ill. IV. Title.
QE861.5.D63 2005
567.9—dc22   2004007307

Acknowledgments
This book was produced for Picture Window Books
by Bender Richardson White, U.K.

Illustrations by James Field (pages 4–5, 11, 19, 21)
and Steve Weston (cover and pages 7, 9, 13, 15, 17).
Diagrams by Stefan Chabluk.
All photographs copyright Digital Vision except
pages 10 and 14 (Corbis Images Inc.).

Consultant: John Stidworthy, Scientific Fellow
of the Zoological Society, London, and former
Lecturer in the Education Department, Natural
History Museum, London.

Reading Adviser: Rosemary G. Palmer, Ph.D.
Department of Literacy, College of Education,
Boise State University, Idaho.

Types of dinosaurs
In this book, a red shape at the top of a left-hand page shows the animal was a meat-eater. A green shape shows it was a plant-eater.

Just how big—or small—were they?
Dinosaurs were many different sizes. We have compared their size to one of the following:

Chicken
2 feet (60 cm) tall
Weight 6 pounds (2.7 kg)

Adult person
6 feet (1.8 m) tall
Weight 170 pounds (76.5 kg)

Elephant
10 feet (3 m) tall
Weight 12,000 pounds
(5,400 kg)

TABLE OF CONTENTS

WHAT'S INSIDE?

Dinosaurs! These dinosaurs lived in the desert. Find out how they survived millions of years ago and what they have in common with today's animals.

LIFE IN THE DESERT

Dinosaurs lived between 230 million and 65 million years ago. The world did not look the same then. The land and seas were not in the same places. Deserts covered much of the land. It was difficult for animals to live in deserts. There was not much water or food for them.

Dinosaurs would search the sand dunes for plants to eat. They would race across the sand, hunting for other dinosaurs, plants, or insects. Other animals such as lizards and little mammals lived there, too.

CARCHARODONTOSAURUS

Carcharodontosaurus was one of the biggest meat-eating dinosaurs. Its sharp teeth could slice easily through its dinosaur meal. Its jaws were big enough to swallow an animal whole.

Sharp teeth and big jaws today

Tigers are large, fierce hunters like the *Carcharodontosaurus* was long ago.

Size Comparison

6

A *Carcharodontosaurus* prowled across the desert, snapping its big teeth.

COELOPHYSIS

Coelophysis hunted in groups. They would all jump on a big animal. They killed with many slashes and bites. In times of drought, food was hard to find. They may have eaten one another just to live.

Gathering to drink today

Antelope gather around water holes in dry weather like *Coelophysis* did millions of year ago.

Size Comparison

Some *Coelophysis* would fight each other for the last bit of water in a water hole.

9

OURANOSAURUS

Pronunciation:
oo-RAN-uh-SAW-rus

Ouranosaurus could walk on all fours or on its back legs. It had a big fin that may have been very colorful. It used its fin to signal to other *Ouranosaurus* in the area.

Attractive colors today

The peacock has a colorful tail like *Ouranosaurus* did long ago.

Size Comparison

An *Ouranosaurus* stood alone in the open desert. Maybe another would see its striped fin and come over.

OVIRAPTOR

Oviraptor's only teeth were a pair in the roof of its mouth. It had a birdlike beak and a crest on its head. An adult *Oviraptor* looked after the eggs in their nests. Many enemies would have wanted to steal the eggs.

A nest today

An ostrich makes a nest to store its eggs just like *Oviraptor* did.

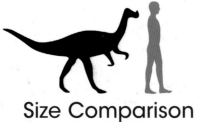

Size Comparison

A mother *Oviraptor* would sit on her nest to keep her eggs warm. She would look out across the desert for enemies.

13

Plateosaurus herds could have gone for days without eating. When they found trees, they stood on their back legs to reach high branches. They pulled down branches with their thumb claws.

Hungry and thirsty today

Camels cross wide deserts like *Plateosaurus* did. They can go for days without food or water.

Size Comparison

A herd of *Plateosaurus* walked across the desert looking for water and food.

PROTOCERATOPS

Pronunciation:
PRO-toe-SAIR-uh-tops

The sandy color of a *Protoceratops* helped them hide in the desert. They had sharp beaks and strong jaws. These helped to cut and chew the tough desert plants.

Moving as a herd today

Zebras live in herds and survive in dry areas like *Protoceratops* did long ago.

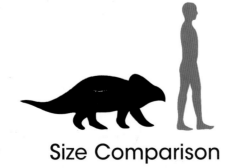

Size Comparison

A herd of *Protoceratops* wandered through the desert. They would search the sand for small plants to eat.

SHUVUUIA

Pronunciation:
SHOO-vu-YOU-ia

Shuvuuia had two tiny arms, each with only one claw. It used the claw for digging in the dry ground. When *Shuvuuia* found worms or insects, snap! It gulped them up in its long, narrow jaws.

Using claws today

Monitor lizards use their claws to find prey like *Shuvuuia* did. They also use them to climb.

Size Comparison

18

With its covering of feathers, a *Shuvuuia* looked like a bird. It even scratched the ground like some birds do.

19

VELOCIRAPTOR

Pronunciation:
veh-LAW-sih-RAP-tur

Velociraptor ran quickly, catching plant-eaters by surprise. It had a huge killing claw on its back foot. *Velociraptor* was covered in feathers like a bird. It looked similar to the *Shuvuuia.*

The chase today

Cheetahs chase their prey at high speed like *Velociraptor* did millions of years ago.

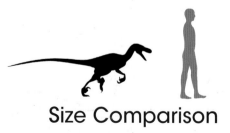

Size Comparison

A *Velociraptor* would hunt in the sand dunes and rocks. It would wait for the chance to attack an unsuspecting dinosaur.

WHERE DID THEY GO?

Dinosaurs are extinct, which means that none of them are alive today. Scientists study rocks and fossils to find clues about what happened to dinosaurs.

People have different explanations about what happened. Some people think a huge asteroid that hit Earth caused all sorts of climate changes. This then caused the dinosaurs to die. Others think volcanic eruptions caused the climate to change and that killed the dinosaurs. No one knows for sure, though.

GLOSSARY

beak—the hard front part of the mouth of birds and some dinosaurs

crest—a structure on top of the head, usually used to signal to other animals

drought—long period with no rain

dunes—hills of sand, mostly found in deserts

herds—large groups of animals that move, feed, and sleep together

mammals—warm-blooded animals that have hair and drink mother's milk when they are young; today's mammals include cats, dogs, rabbits, mice, bears, monkeys, and humans

prey—animals that are hunted by other animals for food; the hunters are known as predators

FIND OUT MORE

AT THE LIBRARY

Dixon, Dougal. *Dinosaur Dig*. Milwaukee, Wis.:
Gareth Stevens Publishing, 2004.

Gray, Samantha, and Sarah Walker. *Dinosaur*.
New York: Dorling Kindersley, 2001.

Lessem, Don. *The Smartest Dinosaurs*.
Minneapolis: Lerner, 2005.

ON THE WEB

FactHound offers a safe, fun way to find Web sites related to this book. All of the sites on FactHound have been researched by our staff.
www.facthound.com

1. Visit the FactHound home page.

2. Enter a search word related to this book, or type in this special code: 1404806679.

3. Click on the Fetch It button.

Your trusty FactHound will fetch the best Web sites for you!

INDEX